W9-CUY-345

Eco-Chic
decorating
GET THE GREEN LIFE

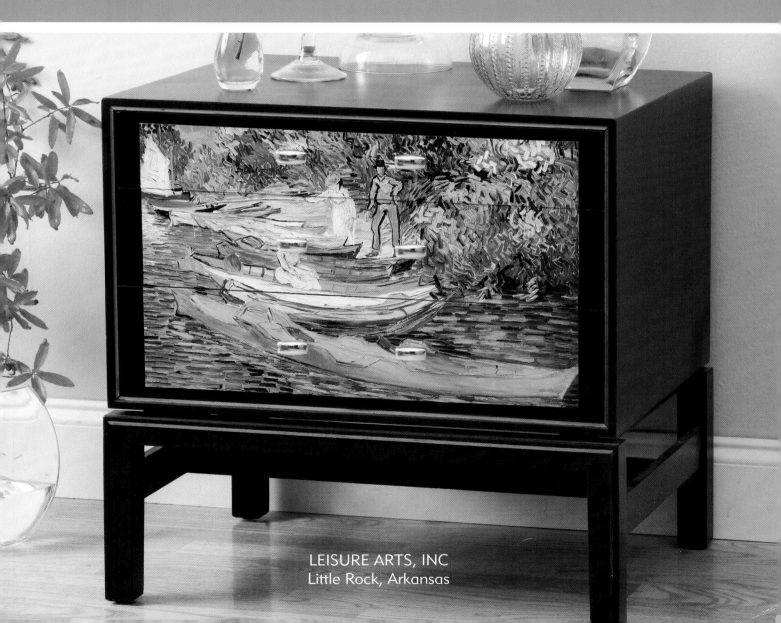

LEISURE ARTS, INC
Little Rock, Arkansas

EDITORIAL
EDITOR-IN-CHIEF: Susan White Sullivan
DESIGNER RELATIONS DIRECTOR: Debra Nettles
CRAFT PUBLICATIONS DIRECTOR: Cheryl Johnson
SPECIAL PROJECTS DIRECTOR: Susan Frantz Wiles
SENIOR PREPRESS DIRECTOR: Mark Hawkins

TECHNICAL
TECHNICAL EDITOR: Lisa Lancaster
TECHNICAL WRITER: Jean Lewis
EDITORIAL WRITER: Susan McManus Johnson

DESIGN
SPECIAL PROJECTS DESIGNER: Patti Uhiren

ART
ART PUBLICATIONS DIRECTOR: Rhonda Shelby
ART CATEGORY MANAGER: Lora Puls
GRAPHIC ARTIST: Angela Ormsby Stark
IMAGING TECHNICIANS: Brian Hall,
    Stephanie Johnson, and Mark R. Potter
PHOTOGRAPHY DIRECTOR: Katherine Laughlin
CONTRIBUTING PHOTOGRAPHER: Mark Mathews
CONTRIBUTING PHOTO STYLIST: Christy Myers
PUBLISHING SYSTEMS ADMINISTRATOR:
    Becky Riddle
PUBLISHING SYSTEMS ASSISTANTS: Clint Hanson,
    John Rose, and Janie Wright

BUSINESS
VICE PRESIDENT AND CHIEF OPERATIONS OFFICER:
    Tom Siebenmorgen
DIRECTOR OF FINANCE AND ADMINISTRATION:
    Laticia Mull Dittrich
VICE PRESIDENT, SALES AND MARKETING: Pam Stebbins
NATIONAL ACCOUNTS DIRECTOR: Martha Adams
SALES AND SERVICES DIRECTOR: Margaret Reinold
INFORMATION TECHNOLOGY DIRECTOR: Hermine Linz
CONTROLLER: Francis Caple
VICE PRESIDENT, OPERATIONS: Jim Dittrich
COMPTROLLER, OPERATIONS: Rob Thieme
RETAIL CUSTOMER SERVICE MANAGER: Stan Raynor
PRINT PRODUCTION MANAGER: Fred F. Pruss

Copyright © 2009 by Leisure Arts, Inc., 5701 Ranch Drive,
Little Rock, AR 72223. All rights reserved. This publication
is protected under federal copyright laws. Reproduction of
this publication or any other Leisure Arts publication,
including publications which are out of print, is prohibited
unless specifically authorized. This includes, but is not
limited to, any form of reproduction or distribution on or
through the Internet, including posting, scanning, or e-mail
transmission. We have made every effort to ensure that these
instructions are accurate and complete. We cannot, however,
be responsible for human error, typographical mistakes, or
variations in individual work. Made in the United States
of America.

Library of Congress Control Number: 2009931390
ISBN-13: 978-1-60140-487-9
ISBN-10: 1-60140-487-5

10 9 8 7 6 5 4 3 2 1

page 71

table of
CONTENTS

page 49

page 120

Save the planet. Save your money. Have fun doing both.

Anyone who can apply tape, use a glue gun, or sew on a button has enough craft knowledge to rescue a huge variety of items that would otherwise be headed for the landfill. In fact, many of the ideas in this book don't require any previous crafting experience at all!

While we worked on these projects, we discovered three different approaches to reaching our ecologically creative goal: Renewing, Reinventing, and Recycling. Each of these ideas takes one or more castoffs and either refreshes their appearance so they can continue in their original use, or recasts them into exciting new roles!

What does this mean for you? By letting these 120+ ideas inspire you, you can have a wide array of "new" furniture, accessories, gifts, and decorator items that only cost you a little time and a few crafting supplies. And they look simply amazing!

Why Eco-Chic Decorating?

Ecology. Even though more of us than ever before are learning about the ways we can recycle in our local communities, the recycling centers and curbside pick-up services we need are not yet available to all areas of the nation. And while new metals, paper, plastic, and glass are often high in recycled content, there are still several materials that are not commonly accepted for recycling anywhere. These include some types of plastic, including rigid and expanded polystyrene (CD cases and foam drinking cups, for example), and some ceramic and glass items such as dishes and window glass.

Economy. We all want to hang on to every spare penny that comes our way. So why buy a new piece of furniture when you can easily renew one to suit your purposes and your décor? And don't hand over big bucks for gifts or organizers until you've had a chance to see how we converted everyday items into new and useful shelves, memo boards, or storage spaces. It just makes good "cents" to reuse!

Style. Not only is recycling the hot topic of the day, it's the hottest trend of decorating. Here are a few of the many ways that refurbished or repurposed items can be fashionable, stylish, and always original: You can make an oversized, elegant ottoman (page 10) from a seen-better-days coffee table. A lovely refreshment bar (page 32) can be quickly crafted from a doorless cabinet. Beautiful napkin rings (page 134) featuring costume jewelry are stunningly easy to make. And retro curtains (page 36) are no-sew simplicity when made from vintage tablecloths.

When you're looking for more storage, new furnishings, or a unique gift, first check your garage and attic or visit flea markets and yard sales. After all, Renewing, Reinventing, and Recycling will always be Eco-Chic!

Here's what furniture manufacturers don't want you to know:

You can save money AND the environment if you skip the home furnishings stores and spend a little time renewing the pieces you already have or the bargains you find in flea markets. Simply by adding some fresh fabrics and paint, your chairs, ottomans, tables, desks, and other furnishings will be ready for many more years of service!

re-NEW

Flea market furnishings can be design classics just as they are. Then again, adding a touch of color or an updated fabric can bridge the decades and put original flair on retro style.

Turn to page 52 to learn how to move a 1950's table and chairs forward in time.

This lamp only needed a touch of silver leaf on the socket, base, and finial for brilliant results. See page 154 to cover the shade with fabric and trim of your choosing.

fifties
FLAIR

It's an ottoman that's large enough to be shared in the family room, yet attractive enough to serve guests in a formal setting.

See page 52 to make your "has-been" coffee table foot-friendly. Our instructions make it easy, so you can take it easy.

all-around FAVORITE

Start with a fabulous ladderback…and give it a style that's right for you. Find your favorite perch on the following pages. With just a little paint and fabric, you'll soon be sitting pretty.

ladderback
SUCCESS

It's a star-spangled glory! Paint the seat red and the chairback slats white. When the slats are dry, apply star stickers and re-paint blue; peel off the stickers when dry.

To put the finishing touches on this All-American Chair, add a purchased cushion and a box pillow (page 53) made from a vintage needlepoint canvas.

Love the frills? To make a chair any girly-girl would adore, add a ruffled cushion, bows, and scenic découpage to a newly painted ladderback. The change begins on page 53. Extraordinary!

A trio of handkerchiefs add a feminine touch to this freshly painted "Rose Bouquet" chair. Hand stitch one to a purchased pillow for a seat cushion; then make a "buttoned-on" chairback cover (page 54). Sweet and easy!

A passion for roses changed this garden-variety nightstand into an accent piece with hybrid appeal. However, any subject that sparks your interest is a fertile topic for a decorative table!

Just paint your nightstand with a crackle finish; then decoupage magazine or catalog clippings to the top. Randomly apply wood-tone spray to give your table an aged appearance. Old-style drawer pulls let you add labels to continue any theme you choose.

everlasting
BLOOMS

An entertainment center moves from the living room to the dining room after its updated transformation. And we didn't spend megabucks for a marble top, either. The secret? Faux marble wallpaper — who knew?

First remove the upper shelving frame, leaving the cabinet part of the unit intact. Then, if your drawer pulls are only ornamental, remove them from the cabinet as well and fill in the holes with wood putty (see **Refinishing Furniture**, page 148, for instructions on preparing furniture for painting). Glue three wooden cutouts to the door fronts and paint the entire cabinet to give the new buffet an equally new style.

Use a brayer to smooth the wallpaper onto the buffet top. Clip the paper at the corners, fold it neatly around the corners, then use craft glue to secure the edges.

at your SERVICE

Tailor a shabby wardrobe with removable door panels into a suitable accessory for any décor. When your new cabinet is complete, you'll be ready to store important items, keep track of time, and jot down the day's menu of events — all in one place!

Turn to page 54 to work this before and after miracle with ease!

a change of WARDROBE

A little sanding along the edges gives this vanilla-toned dining set a timeworn look. Masking off straight lines with painter's tape makes it easy to paint stripes on the chairbacks and drop-leaf table.

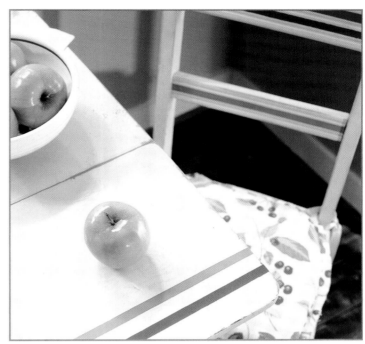

Color is key when uniting flea market furnishings. Crocheted doll-dress potholders, glued to plates, pick up the cheery hues of dish towels in retro prints. Reproduction towels hang from a café curtain rod and accent a pair of seat cushions.

Covering the chair cushions is quick and easy when you hand sew with embroidery floss — just stitch around the cushion, catching ribbon ends in stitching for ties. Trim the excess fabric with pinking shears.

farmhouse MEMORIES

A vintage print puts a pleasant face on this easel-style flea market frame. The simple, timesaving how-to's are on page 55.

Time marches on, leaving us with an abundant supply of artifacts from a century gone by. Using those leftover items to record the passage of time seems like the right thing to do, especially when the one-of-a-kind clocks you create look as good as these.

Old frames are among the items that run the gamut from rustic to regal, and that means countless new timekeeping options for your décor.

Leading a double life can be a good thing — a framed cardboard print does just that after its conversion to a clock/chalkboard. Spend a little time reading the instructions on page 55, then photocopy the design on page 158 to make a noteworthy message center of your own.

a time and a SEASON

There's really no excuse for having plain, boxy furniture — not when it can exhibit this kind of artistic flair! Put your renewed chest on display with poster-decked drawer fronts, sleek knobs, and matching paint.

No fancy brushwork is needed to add this beauty to your collection; just turn to page 56 to learn how to turn a throw-away chest into a masterpiece.

impressive
EXHIBIT

Freshly painted "step" tables are put to work as outdoor end tables on this colorful porch. Top your tables with some eye-catching accessories — the overnight case holds potted plants, and did you notice how lively an ordinary lamp base looks with a crazy new shade? See page 154 to fashion your own wacky lampshade.

To freshen an old sofa cushion, use a bed sheet or length of fabric to wrap it, gift-wrap style. Secure the new cover with big safety pins — so easy!

Sprinkle the outdoor room with bright pillows and re-purposed collectibles (we're especially fond of our clown cookie jar "planter"), and you're ready for a season of fun.

in living COLOR

AT THE
MILLER'S
8:00 PM

When work and play mingle this freely, any task seems easier to tackle!

Black paint rejuvenates the sides, legs, and drawer fronts of this vintage desk. The drawer pulls and plastic inserts get the look of cast aluminum from a touch of silver paint. And surprise! — the refreshing key-lime color at the end of the desk is actually the side of the drawer, painted the happiest tropical shade we could find.

See page 149 to recreate the faux agate desktop in shades of gray.

Every stress-free office should have a patio chair! Black paint refreshes the chair's finish while bark cloth renews the seat cushion.

How-to's on page 56 make covering a round cushion almost effortless, and it's even easier to cover a lampshade with fabric. Just follow the easy directions on page 154.

A few coats of black chalkboard paint changes a framed print (left) into a handy writing surface.

tropic of
DISCUSSION

Freshly hauled from the flea market and missing its doors, this old buffet has definitely seen better days — and yet, its future is bright! Renewed with a little paint and stain, this castoff cabinet will give many more years of service with distinction. A coffee urn turned lamp and purchased baskets complete this redo. See page 56 for the details.

a toast to
TIMELESSNESS

Freedom of expression is a beautiful thing. Turn to page 57 to read about using painter's tape and star-shaped stickers, then let your pride show on your own glorious tabletop!

The role of tables in home décor is usually more functional than decorative, even when their task is to hold an eye-catching centerpiece or elevate a unique lamp. But a flea market table can be as much a focal point as any decorator accent, just by adding color to some or all of its surfaces. Let this trio of bright ideas give you a leg up on the possibilities.

This "mosaic" tabletop isn't tile and it isn't paint — it's paper napkins, cut apart and decoupaged in place. However, the table does wear new paint beneath the artful application. Learn this "tile" technique on page 57.

The dainty table beneath the window wears pretty pinstripes on its top. Painter's tape keeps each line tidy while consecutive paint colors are applied. Turn to page 57 for the easy details.

true COLORS

Use tablecloths to dress a window with no-sew ease! For each curtain, fold the short ends of two same-size tablecloths over a tension rod and secure with safety pins. Tie back the curtains with ribbons.

For the perky valance, no rod is needed! Just fold a square tablecloth into a triangle and use ribbons to tie the triangle ends to nails.

Love the look of linens brightened by bold flowers? Haven't any floral-print linens? Search yard sales, bazaars, and resale shops for the vivid hues that were plentiful in years gone by … you never know when something stunning will crop up!

The window seat (left) is cushioned by a piece of thick foam wrapped in a tablecloth from yesteryear. Safety pins hold the cloth in place.

A ruffled ballon shade, made from a vintage tablecloth, is the focal point for a retro red kitchen. For the how-to's, turn to page 58.

accents made from
CHEERS GONE BY

With second-hand lamps, what you see is often NOT what you get ... and that can be a very good thing! For instance, this white ceramic lamp with fern fronds was obscured under layers of unattractive paint. It took a little scrubbing to restore the lamp base to its original finish, but the results were worth the effort. A scrap of vintage bark cloth (there was just enough to cover the shade!) repeats the natural theme. We share all the lampshade how-to's on page 154.

rather frond of
OLD LAMPS

Fresh as a daisy, our playful patio set beckons you to sit and enjoy a glass of lemonade.

Metal ice cream parlor-style chairs, with removable seats, flank a plant stand turned table base. The tabletop is a wooden circle embellished with paint, ribbon, a round placemat, buttons, artificial flowers and topped with a piece of tempered glass. Turn to page 58 for all the how-to's.

daisy-fresh
PATIO SET

Store your beauty secrets inside your table. If your telephone bench has a built-in planter or tray, you'll find it easy to top with a padded lid. And just in case you're wondering, both the fabric and the pink-and-pretty poodle accessories were lucky flea market finds.

It's the talk of the town — an old telephone bench gets a little polish and becomes a dainty manicure table, yet stays true to its original era with feminine fabric and a pampered poodle collection. Page 59 has all the tips for the easy touch-ups.

well
MANICURED

This old-fashioned tea trolly only needed a coat of silver paint to restore it to its former glory. Now it takes on a new duty—holding your collection of spa essentials.

Refer to **Painting Metal**, page 149, to begin this easy transformation.

The French call them *objects trouvés*, or "found objects." We know exactly what they mean. These vintage vessels were once garage sale bargains.

Silver paint on their lids and stylish stickers made them brand-new bathing beauties – in an instant!

Photocopy our labels on page 160, cut them out and adhere them to your bottles of "bubbly" to add distinction to your *objects trouvés*.

new glamour for
OLD GLASS

For these instant indulgences, search your cabinets and comb secondhand stores for white ware & little luxury linens. What could be more fetching than a trayful of pamper-me pretties, positioned to catch the eye?

Fill an ivory vase or pitcher with brushes. Treat yourself to vanilla-scented candles in tiny teacups — guaranteed to be soothing!

Toss soaps and seashells into a scalloped salad bowl. For splendid hand towels, roll up gently aged dinner napkins and display them in a shallow urn.

Pour bath salts into a gravy boat, then sprinkle spoonfuls of the fragrant crystals into a tub filled with warm water. Now, settle in for a restful soak. With all the time you saved on these easy bath ideas, you can linger as long as you like.

bathing BEAUTY

Can you believe this French-inspired clock began as a Fifties metal tray? We découpaged the flat center with early 20th-century advertisements and a new clock face, *à la Paris*! Can't find any old ads? Use vintage-look scrapbook paper!

A battery-powered clock kit and special longer hands completed this weekend wonder. See page 59 for the how-to's.

Well-traveled trays come in all sizes, shapes, and colors, made from wood, metal, fiberglass, and more! Some have splendid pasts, while others have more humble beginnings, coming from the five-and-dime stores of the 1940's and later. Whatever their origins and present conditions, trays can be easily remade into useful and decorative items.

A plain round metal tray becomes a chic charmer with the addition of paint, bright fabric, and fun trims. A simple wooden folding stand forms the base. Turn to page 60 for the sweet details.

Who would ever guess that the leopard print on this sleek tray was created by using the easy painting technique found on page 60? A wooden folding table or luggage rack makes a handy tray stand.

round tray
3 WAYS

A simple paint technique, page 61, rejuvenates the top of this vintage card table and the backs of the folding chairs with the look of burled wood.

The good life … it's only a picnic away. Invite the best of your memories along by packing your car with some familiar flea market finds: a cooler, a basket, a thermos, and a wooden folding table and chairs. The next time you feel the need to slow down and savor your day, you can make a getaway to the park… and to the good life.

slow down & SAVOR

FIFTIES FLAIR

Pages 8-9

TABLE

The inset on this tabletop is made using mesh-backed sheets of stainless steel tiles. When you use tile sheets, you don't have to place each tile individually.

1. If needed, refer to **Refinishing Furniture**, page 148, to paint or stain your table as desired; allow to dry completely.
2. Following the manufacturer's instructions, use tile mastic to adhere grids of ³/₄" wide stainless steel mosaic tile to the tabletop; allow surface to dry overnight.
3. Working in small sections, use a rubber grout float to apply grey, pre-mixed, sanded grout to the tile surface in an even layer.

4. Using a grout sponge and working at a 45-degree angle, continue wiping the table top until all excess grout has been removed.

CHAIRS

1. Remove the chair seats. If needed, refer to **Refinishing Furniture**, page 148 to prepare the chairs for painting. Spray paint the chairs brown; allow to dry completely.
2. Following the manufacturer's instructions, apply silver leaf to the chair backs.
3. Refer to page 153 to cover the chair seats with your choice of fabric.

ALL-AROUND FAVORITE

Pages 10-11

1. If needed, refer to **Refinishing Furniture**, page 148, to prepare your table base for painting.
2. Prime, then paint base with desired color. Allow to dry completely.
3. Cut a piece of thick foam the size of the tabletop.
4. For the fabric cover, measure the diameter of the tabletop and add 12". Cut a square of fabric the determined measurement.
5. Divide the diameter measurement from Step 4 in half and add 9". Tie one end of a length of string to a pen. Insert a thumbtack through the string at the determined measurement. Fold the fabric square in half from top to bottom and again from left to right. Insert the thumbtack through the folded corner of the fabric and use the pen to draw a cutting line as shown in Fig. 1. Cut along drawn line through all layers; unfold cover.

Fig. 1

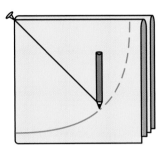

6. Cut a piece of batting slightly smaller than the fabric piece.

7. Center the foam, then the table (upside down) on the batting. Pull the batting taut and smooth. Working alternately on opposite sides of the table, staple the batting to the underside of the tabletop, folding the batting to ease in place. If necessary, trim excess batting from the bottom of the tabletop.

8. Center the tabletop on the wrong side of the fabric cover. Repeat Step 7 to staple the fabric cover in place.

9. Using T-pins to hold fringe in place as you go, hot glue bullion fringe along the bottom edge of the tabletop, then glue decorative trim along the top of the bullion fringe.

LADDERBACK SUCCESS
Pages 12-15

ALL AMERICAN CHAIR
Box Pillow
Use ¹/₂" seam allowances for all sewing.

1. For the pillow front, trim your stitched piece ¹/₂" larger on all sides than the desired size of pillow.

2. For a pillow form, cut a piece of thick foam (ours measures 2³/₄" thick) 1" smaller in each direction than the pillow front.

3. For the pillow back, cut a piece of fabric the same size as the front.

4. For the pillow sides, measure the circumference and depth of the foam, then add 1" to each measurement. Cut a strip of fabric the determined measurements, piecing if necessary. With right sides together, stitch short ends of side strip together; press the seam allowance open.

5. Follow **Welting**, page 150, to make and attach covered welting to the pillow front and back.

6. Sew the side strip to the pillow front. Leaving an opening for turning and inserting the pillow form, sew the remaining raw edge of the side strip to the pillow back. Hand sew the opening closed.

GIRLY-GIRL CHAIR

1. If needed, refer to **Refinishing Furniture**, page 148, to prepare your chair for painting. Paint the chair white, then paint the desired sections of the rungs and spindles black.

2. Cut fabric strips from toile fabric and use découpage glue to adhere the strips to selected sections of the spindles and allow to dry. To seal the fabric, apply two addtional coats of glue over the fabric.

3. For welting and ruffle length, measure from one spindle, across the seat front, to the other spindle. To make welting, follow **Making Welting**, page 150. To make ruffle, follow **Ruffle**, page 150.

4. Baste welting to the right side of the seat cover top from one spindle mark to the other. Baste ruffle to right side of seat cover top over welting.

5. Matching right sides and leaving an opening for turning, sew seat cover top and bottom together. Turn right side out and hand sew the opening closed.

6. If desired, sew a length of ribbon to each back corner of the seat cover. Tie the ribbon ends into a bow around the spindles to secure the seat cover

ROSE BOUQUET CHAIR

3. To add bows, drill two holes about three inches apart in each slat. Thread lengths of ribbon through the holes; tie the ribbon into bows at the front.

Seat Cover
1. Use kraft paper to make a pattern of the chair seat (drawing around the spindles). Add a ½" seam allowance.
2. Using the pattern, cut one seat cover top and one bottom.

1. Paint the chair white, then paint the desired sections of the rungs, slats, and spindles yellow.

2. To make the chairback cover, match wrong sides and sew three buttons through the top edges of two same-sized handkerchiefs.

3. Drape the cover over the chairback.

A CHANGE OF WARDROBE
Pages 20-21

1. If needed, refer to **Refinishing Furniture**, page 148, to prepare your wardrobe cabinet for painting.

2. Remove any mirrors, door backing panels, and knobs or handles. Use wood glue to adhere wood cutouts to the drawer fronts, then paint the cabinet. Attach new knobs.

3. To make the chalkboard, follow manufacturer's instructions to paint one door backing panel with chalkboard paint, then reinstall it. If your cabinet does not have backing panels in the doors, you can cut pieces of plywood to fit the door openings.

4. To make the clock, you will need a round wooden plate that fits on one door panel and a clock kit. Refer to page 149 to learn more about clock parts.

5. Paint the plate black.

6. Sizing to fit your plate, make a color photocopy of the clock face on page 159 and cut it out. Use spray adhesive to mount the clock face on the plate. Drill a hole through the center of the plate large enough for the clock shaft. Center and drill the same size hole in the door panel.

7. Draw around the panel on the wrong side of a piece of fabric; cut fabric out 2" outside the drawn line. Use spray adhesive to adhere the fabric to the panel. Cut an X through the fabric at the drilled hole, then follow the manufacturer's instructions to install the clock movement module and hands. Reinstall the door panel in the cabinet.

A TIME AND A SEASON
Pages 24-25

EASEL CLOCK

1. Paint an easel frame with green acrylic paint, then apply a fruitwood gel stain with a cloth; wipe off the excess.

2. Use a gold metallic rub-on finish to add accents to the frame.

3. Cut a piece of mat board to fit in the frame. Use spray adhesive to adhere an old print to the board for the clock face.

4. Turn to page 149 to learn about clock parts. Drill a hole through the clock face, then follow the manufacturer's instructions to install a clock movement module and hands. Adhere self-adhesive numerals to the clock face, and secure it in the frame.

CLOCK CHALKBOARD

1. Remove a cardboard print from its frame, spray the print with gray primer, then apply two or three coats of black chalkboard paint.

Note: If you have a frame that does not have a cardboard print, you can make the chalkboard from a piece mat board cut to fit your frame.

2. Sizing as needed to fit the top portion of your board, make a photocopy of the clock face on page 158. Use spray adhesive to adhere the face to the board.

3. Turn to page 149 to learn about clock parts. Drill a hole through the center of the clock face, then follow the manufacturer's instructions to install a clock movement module and hands. Secure the board in the frame.

4. To separate the clock from the chalkboard, paint a thin piece of wooden trim to match the frame and glue it just below the bottom edge of the clock face.

IMPRESSIVE EXHIBIT

Pages 26-27

1. To prepare the chest for painting, remove any knobs or handles, then refer to **Refinishing Furniture**, page 148, if needed.
2. Prime, then paint the chest.
3. Align the drawer fronts, then measure the area where the poster will be placed; trim the poster to the determined measurements.
4. Aligning the drawer fronts, use spray adhesive to adhere the poster to the drawer fronts, then use a straight edge and sharp craft knife to cut the poster between each drawer. Apply brush-on sealer along the edges of the poster to secure.
5. Attach new knobs or handles to the drawers.

TROPIC OF DISCUSSION

Pages 30-31

Use ¹/₂" seam allowances.

1. For a pillow form, measure the diameter of the chair seat, then cut a circle of thick foam the determined measurement.
2. Add 1" to the measurement and cut two circles of fabric for the cushion top and bottom.
3. For the pillow sides, measure the circumference and depth of the pillow form, then add 1" to each measurement. Cut a strip of fabric the determined measurements, piecing if necessary.
4. With right sides together, stitch short ends of side strip together; press seam open. Follow **Welting**, page 150, to make and attach welting to the top and bottom.
5. Matching right sides, sew the side strip to the pillow top. Leaving an opening for turning and inserting the pillow form, sew the side strip to the pillow bottom.
6. Turn the pillow cover right side out and insert the pillow form. Hand sew the opening closed.

A TOAST TO TIMELESSNESS

Pages 32-33

1. Refer to **Refinishing Furniture**, page 148, for tips on preparing your buffet for painting.
2. Paint the top of the buffet red and the base cream.
3. Using water-based stain and wiping away the excess with a soft cloth while the stain is still wet, apply a walnut stain to the top of the buffet and a pine stain to the base. To add highlights, dampen a cloth and continue to wipe over selected areas, removing excess stain until the desired look is achieved.
4. Refer to **Covering Foam Core Or Poster Board With Fabric**, page 151, to make fabric-covered side panels. Glue the side panels to the buffet.

LAMP

1. Use household cement to adhere a small silver candlestick lamp to the inverted lid of a coffee urn.

2. Snip the lip of the lid at the back, then bend the metal into a V-shape to make a groove for the cord to rest safely.

3. Add a clip-on black bell lampshade for a distinctive flair.

TRUE COLORS
Pages 34-35

FLAG SOFA TABLE

1. If needed, refer to **Refinishing Furniture**, page 148, to prepare your table for painting. Paint the entire table white and allow it to dry.

2. To create a field for the stars, tape off a section in the upper left corner with painter's tape. Arrange large star stickers within the taped border, making sure the edges adhere well so the top color does not bleed under them. Sponge paint the star field blue and allow it to dry overnight. Carefully remove the stickers and tape.

3. Using the edge of the table as the first stripe, and spacing stripes evenly from front to back, tape off the flag's stripes and sponge paint them red. When dry, carefully remove the tape.

MOSAIC "TILED" TABLE

1. If needed, refer to **Refinishing Furniture**, page 148, to prepare your table for painting. Paint the entire table white and allow it to dry. Paint the bottom portion of your table, then the tabletop with coordinating paint colors (your tabletop color will become the "grout" between your paper napkin "tiles"). A light color of paint for the grout works best, as the decopaged napkins will become translucent.

2. Cut the borders from cocktail napkins, then separate the plies. Using only the top ply and starting from the middle and working outward, position the napkin centers and border pieces on the tabletop, leaving a space between each piece.

3. Using Aleene's® Paper Appliqué glue, adhere the napkin pieces to the tabletop. Apply several coats of glue over the entire tabletop to seal the surface.

PINSTRIPE TABLE

Allow paint and primer to dry between coats.

1. If needed, refer to **Refinishing Furniture**, page 148, to prepare your table for painting. Paint the entire table white and allow it to dry.

2. To make the stripes we used three colors of paint in addition to the base coat of white.

3. Use painter's tape to mask off stripes as desired on the table top (our stripes vary in width and the colors are randomly placed).

4. Paint the stripes with the lightest color.

5. Remove tape and then mask off stirpes for second color. Repeat to add third color.

ACCENTS MADE FROM CHEERS GONE BY

Pages 36-37

1. To make the shade, measure the inside width of your window and multiply by two; measure the height of your window and add ten inches. If your tablecloth is close to the width measurement, use it as is to avoid hemming the sides. Otherwise, cut your tablecloth the determined measurements and make a 1/2" hem along each side edge.

2. Press the top edge of the tablecloth 41/4" to the wrong side; stitch across the top of the tablecloth 4" from the pressed edge; topstitch again 21/2" from the pressed edge to make a casing.

3. For the ruffle, measure the width of the shade and multiply by two; cut a piece of fabric 51/2" wide by the determined measurement, piecing as necessary. Make a 1/2" hem along one long edge (bottom) of ruffle.

4. Baste 1/8" and 1/4" from the raw edge of the ruffle. Pull the basting threads to gather the ruffle to fit the bottom edge of the shade. Matching the right sides and raw edges, pin the ruffle to the bottom edge of the shade; use a 1/2" seam allowance to sew the ruffle to the shade.

5. Insert a tension rod through casing; mount rod at the top of your window, allowing 2" at top for the header. Cut two lengths of ribbon the length of the shade. Drape ribbons over rod, around to the back of the shade, and pin or tie the ends together to create the balloon effect.

DAISY-FRESH PATIO SET

Pages 40-41

1. Remove the seats from the chairs. Refer to **Painting Metal**, page 149, to prime and paint the chairs, plant stand, and tabletop.

2. Follow **Covering A Chair Seat**, page 153, to cover the seats with fabric.

3. Glue ribbon around the edge of the tabletop. Glue a round placemat to the center of the tabletop.

4. Remove the stems and centers from a variety of artificial flowers, then glue the flower petals and some coordinating buttons to the tabletop.

5. Use cable clips (found in the wiring section of hardware stores) to attach the tabletop to the plant stand. Cover the tabletop with a piece of polished-edge tempered glass.

WELL MANICURED
Pages 42-43

1. Remove the seat, then refer to **Painting Metal**, page 149, to prime and paint the telephone bench white; allow to dry.

2. For the padded tray lid, cut a piece of 1" thick foam the same size as the outer measurements of the tray opening. Cut a piece of batting and fabric 2" larger on all sides than foam piece. Cut two pieces of 1/4" thick foam core 1/2" smaller on all sides than foam piece; stack and glue the foam core pieces together.

3. Center the batting, then the foam on the wrong side of the fabric piece. Pulling the fabric taut, wrap and glue the center of two opposite edges of fabric to the bottom of the foam. Continue wrapping the fabric over the foam, folding the ends gift-wrap style and gluing in place as you go.

4. Draw around foam core stack on the wrong side of fabric; cut a piece of fabric 2" larger on all sides than foam core. Center the foam core on the wrong side of the fabric piece. Follow Step 3 to cover the foam core piece with fabric.

5. Matching wrong sides, center and glue foam core piece on foam piece. Working on a hard surface, use hammer and awl to punch a hole through center of padded lid; attach a knob to the lid using a long screw.

6. To cover the original seat with fabric, draw around the seat on the wrong side of fabric; cut out fabric 3" outside the drawn line. Fold the ends of the fabric gift-wrap style around the base of the seat and staple them in place.

7. Cut a piece of poster board 1/2" smaller than the seat. Cut a piece of fabric 1" larger on all sides than the poster board. Follow Step 6 to cover poster board with fabric. Matching wrong sides, glue poster board to the bottom of the seat.

ROUND TRAY THREE WAYS
Pages 48-49

TRAY CLOCK
Allow paint and primer to dry between coats.

1. Drill a hole through the center of a round metal tray to fit a purchased clock kit. Turn to page 149 to learn more about clock parts.

2. Sand tray, then apply primer to the entire tray. Paint the outer edges of the tray bottom ivory.

3. Apply a clear spray sealer to the front and back of advertisement pages from old books or scrapbook paper. Applying glue only to the center of the tray, and overlapping and trimming as desired, follow découpage glue manufacturer's instructions to adhere the pages or scrapbook paper to the center of the tray; allow to dry.

4. Use a craft knife to trim the edges of the pages even with the edges of the tray center.

5. Make a photocopy of the clock face on page 159, enlarging or reducing as necessary to fit your tray. Cut out the clock face; apply sealer to both sides of the photocopy. Découpage the clock face to the center of the tray.

6. To age the clock, apply a brown gel stain to the découpaged area of the clock, then wipe with a soft cloth to remove excess stain. Lightly spray the clock with wood-tone spray.

7. Apply a bronze metallic rub-on finish along the rim and edges of the clock face. Seal the entire clock with clear varnish.

8. Follow manufacturer's instructions to attach a clock movement module and hands to the tray (we purchased a set of longer hands to fit our clock).

CHIC CHARMER TRAY
Allow primer and paint to dry between coats.

1. Sand tray and stand; apply primer. Paint tray white and stand pink.

2. Cut a circle of fabric to fit in the center bottom of the tray. Use spray adhesive to glue the fabric circle to the tray.

3. Use craft or fabric glue to adhere a decorative trim to cover the raw edges of the fabric. Glue jumbo rickrack around the rim of the tray.

4. Place tray on stand.

LEOPARD PRINT TRAY
Allow primer and paint to dry between coats.

1. Sand tray, then apply primer to the tray. Paint the rim black and the center light beige. **Note:** More than one coat of paint may be need for even coverage.

2. For the leopard spots, refer to the photo below to paint medium brown dots in various sizes and shapes on the center of the tray. Paint dark brown uneven lines along the edges of the spots.

3. Apply a brown gel stain to the center of the tray, then wipe with a soft cloth to remove excess stain.

4. Apply an antique gold metallic rub-on finish to the rim, then apply two coats of sealer to the entire tray.

5. Place tray on stand.

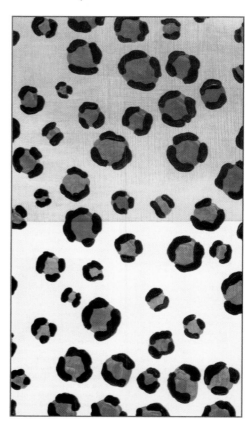

SLOW DOWN AND SAVOR

Pages 50-51

Create the look of burled wood on a weathered wooden card table and chairs. Our table has a picturesque scene, which we chose to accentuate by only painting the table edges.

1. Use painter's tape to mask along the edges of the center square. Apply a coat of light brown paint to the entire outer border area. Dry Brush, page 148, the painted area with antique metallic gold paint.

2. To paint the light brown side sections, mix an equal amount of light colored gel wood stain with clear acrylic glaze; brush the mixture over the surface. Press a small damp sponge into the wet mixture; twist and lift straight up, creating a circular pattern. Overlap circles and vary the amount of pressure on the sponge.

3. Repeat Step 2 to paint the dark brown corners with a mixture of dark gel stain and glaze. Allow the paint to cure.

4. For the decorative gold lines, place strips of painter's tape ⅛" apart along the edges of the painted sections. Apply a gold metallic rub-on finish between the strips of tape, allow to dry, then remove the tape.

5. For the chairs, choose the areas on the chair backs you wish to accentuate and repeat Steps 1-4.

6. Seal the table and chairs with a water-based polyurethane varnish.

Okay, so you really aren't too wild about that garage-sale coffee table anymore.

However, by thinking Eco-Chic, you realize you can keep it out of the landfill by reinventing it. When the change is complete, you have an exciting new bench! This idea and dozens more will help you find fresh ways to use old furniture, dishes, linens, and more.

re-INVENT

LIFE

U.S. PILOT'S WIFE

DECEMBER 20, 1943 **10** CENTS
YEARLY SUBSCRIPTION $4.50

Dining alfresco? Don't forget your luggage! This 20th century valise is actually a picnic table, complete with dinnerware inside!

The fold-out legs snap into place, converting the aluminum-framed case into an instant tabletop. A sheet of tempered glass makes a regular fixture of this portable find.

a case of restated IDENTITY

Restore the stand of an old washtub with white rustproof paint. Then fill the tub with ice and summer treats.

Or create a cozy table-and-chair combination by topping your washtub with a window sash. Overlay the sash with a sheet of tempered glass for a smooth dining surface. Complete the set with a pair of white wooden chairs, accented with red paint-marker dots.

It's the earliest of washing machines, minus two important working parts — a pair of chapped hands! Celebrate your freedom from the days of hand-scrubbed laundry by converting an old washtub into something fun!

rub-a-dub
TUB

Want to refashion an old wooden desk into a youthful new workspace for an artist on the rise? See page 108 to brighten your desk with a little paint and striped fabric.

Above, a purchased pair of pre-covered photo boxes tidies up the desk shelves. Cover the box lids (see page 151) with your leftover fabric scraps — decorating can be child's play!

Corkboard sheets replace the glass in a salvaged window, creating a fun bulletin board with versatile mini segments. Search the button box for multi-colored buttons and glue them to jumbo push-pins to keep up with key items like notes, stickers, and jewelry. See the how-to's on page 108.

It's elementary! Chalkboard paint turns the sides of these flea market tins into writing surfaces. Top off the look by painting the lids with the same playful colors used on the desk and bulletin board. Be sure to apply primer to your tins before painting.

young at
ART

Are you smiling? These flea market cameras represent thirty-six years of snapshot history. Purchased frames are glued over the lens windows and inside the flash reflector. A little black paint and an application of a silver rub-on finish and no one will ever know these frames were not original to the cameras.

When photography was new, "getting your picture made" was an elaborate production that yielded stuffy photos of somber subjects. The tradition of smiling for the camera probably didn't begin until the 1920's, when anyone could own and use inexpensive cameras like the Brownie. The opening in the side of this Argus® Seventy-five camera case holds a purchased wire photo tree, a nice way to display your own candid photos.

snappy photo DISPLAYS

To put guests at ease, you need more than a simple welcome mat in your entryway. This attractive foyer (opposite) gets its appeal from an inviting table-turned-bench. This is a graceful transition you can easily achieve by following the directions on page 108.

Instantly convert a rattan end table (above) into a cozy seat by wrapping decorator fabric around foam and plywood cut to fit your tabletop. Staple the fabric to the bottom of the wood for a quick, no-sew fix-up. To make your little bench the best seat in the house, top it with coordinating pillows.

turn the
TABLES

A dilapidated dresser or chest of drawers can give rise to many creative projects. Turn that too-good-to-resist flea market find into a trendy necessity for a den or living room.

For our drawer turned ottoman, we wrapped batting and fabric around thick foam and tucked it inside the drawer. Recycled turned wooden legs add height and understated elegance. Turn to page 109, for all the details, then prop up your feet in comfort.

A deep wooden drawer gets a "lift" from wooden finials to become a helpful book box. Simply stain the finials and all the drawer surfaces, inside and out, to match the drawer front. Then use wood glue or screws to attach one finial to each corner of the drawer.

simply
SOPHISTICATED

Money may not grow on trees, but your memories can!

This curlicued photo holder may remind you of a lovely garden trellis — but would you believe its origin is even more "entrancing"? At one time, these decorative swirls and the faded bluebird at their center formed a protective barrier for a screen door. Now they rise up from a can filled with floral foam to become a whimsical memory tree. A gingham ribbon and artificial greenery wind around the base of the tree, and a half-dozen snapshots dangle from bow-tied clothespins.

picture
THIS

Your bedroom should be the most comfortable — and comforting — space in the house. Dress your bed with plump pillows and soft linens, making it a cozy spot to relax.

For an unexpected touch of romance, convert a wire-mesh fireplace screen into a wall-mounted headboard with fabric-covered panels. See page 109 for the easy instructions. And while you're in the makeover mode, why not complete several sets of the panels in fabrics to change with the seasons? You'll have the time, because this easy project can be completed in a weekend — or less!

hearth to
HEADBOARD

Flea market shoppers know that everything old can be new again, especially when those out-dated items are given fresh, contemporary style. Before, form clashes with function when it comes to this trio of drab lamps … the truth is, they look much better in the dark! After, without the wiring, the lamp bases become original candlesticks that will brighten any setting. Turn to page 110 for all the details.

true
ENLIGHTENMENT

Family photos and antique linens come together to form a charming link to the past. The cloth overlay on this ready-made album was cut from an embroidered pillowcase. Page 110 has the easy instructions.

Add a personal touch to your address book and journal using snippets cut from a lace doily or pretty hankie. If your book has a printed cover, don't worry! Simply glue card stock over the printed area. Turn to page 110 for the complete instructions.

on the
COVER

A small, plain shade blossoms in an instant with a delicate handkerchief cover. Just cut the hankie in half and fold a hem along each cut edge. To gather, thread a needle with narrow ribbon and sew a running stitch near the folded edge of each piece, leaving long ribbon ends. Draping both halves of the hankie over the shade, tie the ribbon ends into a bow at each side.

A teacup or a goblet is the perfect feminine base for one of these dainty lampshades. Simply position a battery-operated candlestick lamp securely in your collectible and fill in around the candlestick with pearls, moss, or silk flower petals.

as pretty
DOES

A bleeding heart finds joy again! Its new cachepot is a flea-market coal scuttle with a fresh "lining" of fuschia acrylic paint.

Tired of topiaries? Irked by ivy? Maybe it's not the plant that's making you itch for something different — it could be the planter. Here's our fun cure for gardener's regret: Combine the most offbeat of secondhand containers with the most surprising of paint colors. Now you've got playful planters with presence and pizzazz. It's enough to make a weeping ficus smile.

Round stickers and bright colors of acrylic paint (see page 111) spread delightful dots around the rims of a quartet of clay flowerpots. Fresh paint jazzes up the interior of the old toolbox, too.

A windowpane-embossed Mason jar becomes a playful vase when wrapped in an antique handkerchief. Secure the handkerchief with a one-of-a-kind earring.

playful
PLANTERS

By painting a wire freezer basket (opposite) and giving it a bright ribbon and a silk posy, we fashioned a bath caddy that's worthy of an expensive spa. Refer to **Painting Metal**, page 149, for the how-to's.

The same technique also worked on an old wine rack — we just sanded its edges after applying a fresh coat of paint. Create your own bathtime convenience with these before and after ideas. You deserve the luxury!

matters of
CONVENIENCE

Turn a lid-less sugar bowl and a necklace into a romantic hanging candleholder — in an instant! See page 111 for the easy directions.

Even without their stoppers, crystal decanters (opposite) can offer refreshing style. Bottle-adapter lamp kits, sprayed with chrome paint, give these decanters a second life. And plain lampshades go posh when covered in fabric and edged with tasseled or beaded fringe. Turn to page 154 for the easy lampshade directions. Supporting the crystal clear theme are a cut glass luncheon plate and a silver-plated tray.

crystal
CLEAR

An outdoor gathering gets quick but formal lighting with the combination of an old chandelier and a garden urn. Remove the wiring from the chandelier, then sand away the worst of the rust. Dry brush the chandelier and urn (page 148) with antique white paint, allowing some of the rust to show through. Fill the urn with floral foam and moss, then secure the chandelier to the foam with wire. Simply elegant!

lightening your MOOD

Orphaned stemware and china are easy-to-find and usually inexpensive resale items. Here a goblet, teapot, sugar dish, and teacup take on new duties as charming vases. Grouping these "misfits" together on a large tray turns them into an eyecatching centerpiece.

One of the benefits of flea market shopping is the license for creativity — when you pay less than retail for wonderful things, you feel free to use your purchases in unique ways. Glassware is a shining example of how an old form can sparkle in a new function.

For a healthier glow, toss out the candy in favor of candlelight! Castoff candy dishes make radiant candleholders, especially when filled with candle gel. Ribbon and an earring help sweeten the mix. Never worked with candle gel before? It's an easy-to-use candlemaking supply you can find at your local hobby store. Refer to **Making Candles**, page 155, to learn more about working with candle gel.

The hollow pedestal of an overturned cake stand becomes a charming little vase. Circling the pedestal are rose-scented candles in matching votive cups.

fabulous
FINDS

To showcase an heirloom photograph, trim a black-and-white photocopy to fit the center of a small dessert plate, then attach it with spray adhesive. Use plate hangers or stands to display your unique frames.

Here's a time traveler with a new twist! Transforming a china tidbit tray into a distinctive clock couldn't be simpler.

Just replace the handle in the center of the tray with an inexpensive battery-powered clock movement. Readily available at most craft and hobby stores, the clock movements are easy to install. Turn to page 149 to learn more about clock parts. Imagine the possibilities!

Mount your creation on a wall using the hanger on the clock movement or display it on a classic easel.

more time for OLD CHINA

This "bowl-me-over" table couldn't be simpler to create. A stack of enamelware bowls makes a sturdy pedestal for a tabletop of tempered glass. Double-stick foam mounting tape secures the bowls without damaging their surfaces.

Revive the neighborly days of back-porch visits by adding a touch of nostalgia to your outdoor décor. Fold-down steps on this old step stool (top left) make it an instant multi-level table. New paint freshens its look, while an overturned tray widens the top step.

Think outside the box to make your outdoor spaces fresh and happy. By repurposing what you already have, some old items can even serve double duty. A suitcase on an old bench is not only a place for your glass of iced tea, it also serves as storage for a book and a light blanket for leisurely moments on the porch. Add some fresh paint and fabric, and "everything old is new again."

neighborly
SPACES

It's all within your reach...especially when you use a ladder! If you need to organize a lot of items in a small space, think vertical. An old wooden ladder is great for elevating everything from egg beaters to cookbooks. Check garage sales as well as flea markets for these vintage decorating accessories.

Single-handle baskets, designed for hanging, transform this castoff ladder into a hardworking clutter-catcher. Wire-edged cotton ribbon bows secure the baskets to the rungs.

storage,
STRAIGHT UP!

When searching for a unique container for fresh cut flowers, one item you don't want to overlook is the insulated beverage bottle. When its days of serving temperature-perfect beverages are over, re-cycle it into a cheerful vase!

Delight your friends with gifts of flowers from your garden arranged in eye-catching containers. These little blossoms have a big impact when presented in enamelware mugs. Add an extra special touch when you tie a photocopy of one of the floral gift tags from page 156, to your present.

gifts from the
GARDEN

Sweet in so many ways, handkerchief sachets are also simple to create! Bundle your favorite potpourri in a muslin square, then wrap it in a vintage hankie and tie with coordinating ribbons. Insert the stem of a silk blossom between the gathers and you are finished! So easy and quick, you'll want to make several — for yourself and to use as gifts.

gifts of good
SCENTS

Heart-shaped aluminum molds form the clever basis for the "giftable" sweetheart candles shown here. So easy — just add melted wax and wicks to the molds and allow the wax to harden. Turn to **Making Candles**, page 155, to learn more about working with wax.

Package each candle in clear plastic wrap and tie with a pretty ribbon; attach a simple handcrafted tag made from cardstock and decorative paper.

gifts from the
HEART

YOUNG AT ART
Pages 68-69

FABRIC-COVERED DESK

1. If needed, refer to **Refinishing Furniture**, page 148, to prepare your desk for painting.

2. Paint entire desk your favorite color. Using one or more coordinating colors, paint selected areas of the desk (we painted the decorative spindles on the legs and the drawer pull).

3. Cut a coordinating stripe fabric into pieces large enough to cover and fold around the desktop and drawer fronts. Pulling fabric taunt and folding neatly at the corners, staple the excess fabric to the underside of the desktop and the wrong side of the drawer fronts. Install drawer pulls.

4. To protect the desktop fabric, you can have a piece of tempered glass cut to fit the desktop.

WINDOW BULLETIN BOARD

1. Working from the wrong side of the window, carefully remove the glass panes.

2. On the front, paint the inside edges of each pane section a different color.

3. Cut a piece of cork and foam core to fit inside each opening. Use spray adhesive to adhere the cork to the foam core. Working from the wrong side, use glazier points or tacks to secure a cork board in each opening.

4. For a backing, cut a piece of foam core slightly smaller than the window. Glue or nail the backing to the wrong side of the window.

TURN THE TABLES
Pages 72-73

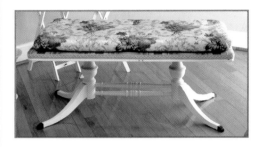

1. If needed, refer to **Refinishing Furniture**, page 148, to prepare your table for painting. Paint the entire table the color you desire.

2. Measure the width and length of your tabletop. Cut several pieces of quilt batting this measurement. Cut a piece of fabric 2" larger in each direction than the batting pieces.

3. Layer the batting and fabric on the tabletop. Working alternately along the long sides, and pulling the fabric taunt as you go, glue the edges of the fabric to the edges of the table. Mitering the corners, glue the fabric edges to the short sides of the table. Trim any excess fabric even with the edge of the table. Glue decorative trim over the raw edges of the fabric.

4. For the cushion, cut a piece of thick foam to fit the top of your table. Cut a piece of fabric large enough to wrap around the foam and overlap slightly at the bottom. Wrap the foam, gift-wrap style with the fabric. Sew or safety-pin the overlapped edges together.

5. To tuft the cushion, evenly spacing the tufts and pulling thread taunt to cinch the foam, sew a decorative button to the top and a flat button to the bottom of the cushion.

SIMPLY SOPHISTICATED
Pages 74-75

DRAWER OTTOMAN
Allow paint and wood-tone spray to dry between coats.

1. If needed, refer to **Refinishing Furniture**, page 148, to prepare your drawer for painting.

2. Paint the entire drawer and legs with a dark brown base coat. Add a light colored topcoat and then glaze with a glossy wood-tone spray. Sand the surface randomly to reveal the underlying paint layers.

3. Use wood glue or screws to attach one leg to each corner of the drawer.

4. Place a thick piece of foam in the bottom of the drawer for height. Refer to **Making A Cushion With Foam And Fabric**, page 152, to wrap another piece of foam with batting and fabric. Place the cushion on top of the foam in the drawer.

HEARTH TO HEADBOARD
Pages 78-79

An easy-to-find flea market fireplace screen can be the focal point of your bedroom when made into a padded panel headboard. Just cover mat board with batting and fabric to fit in the screen sections.

1. To make patterns for panels, lay each screen section down on kraft paper and draw along the inner edges.

2. For each panel, use the pattern to cut one piece each of mat board and felt.

3. Draw around the pattern on batting and on the wrong side of fabric. Cut out batting piece one inch outside and fabric piece two inches outside the drawn lines.

4. To cover each panel, center batting piece, then mat board piece, on the wrong side of fabric piece. Fold and then use fabric glue to adhere the edges of the fabric to the back of the mat board, folding fabric to ease it in place along the edges of the curves.

5. Glue the felt piece to the back of the panel, concealing the fabric edges.

6. Slip the fabric-covered panels under the edges of the metal frame. Hot glue panels in place for a permanent decoration or use a needle and thread to tack panels to screen from the back for easy removal, so you can change panels with the seasons.

TRUE ENLIGHTENMENT
Pages 80-81

Our lamp bases have either a crackle finish (above) or a distressed look (below).

1. Remove all electrical hardware from the lamp bases. Some lamp bases will be in several separate pieces once the hardware is removed; use household cement to glue the pieces together, if needed.

2. For a distressed look, prime, paint, then sand the lamp bases. For a crackle finish, prime, paint, then follow the manufacturer's instructions to apply crackle medium.

3. To soften the look of either of the painting techniques, apply a water-based stain then wipe away the excess while still wet.

4. Glue saucers or small plates to the top to hold the candles. Add decorative trim, tassels, or bows if desired.

ON THE COVER
Pages 82-83

JOURNAL AND ADDRESS BOOK

1. If desired, use decorative-edge scissors to cut a piece of cardstock slightly smaller than the front cover of your journal or address book. Glue the cardstock to the cover.

2. Allowing about 1/2" extra fabric on each edge for wrapping around the top and side edges of the cover, cut a corner from a handkerchief slightly smaller than the cover or cardstock.

3. Allowing the decorative edge to peek out, glue the hankie to the cover or cardstock. Fold the top and side raw edges to the inside of the cover.

4. For a finished look, glue lengths of ribbon or decorative trim over the raw edges of the hankie.

5. To close the book, glue two lengths of ribbon to the inside edge of the back cover. Sew or glue a button to the edge of the front cover; tie the ribbon around the button.

PHOTO ALBUM

1. Allowing about 1/2" extra fabric on each edge for wrapping around the top, bottom, and side edges of the cover, cut the decorative border from an embroidered pillowcase.

2. Center the decorative edge on the front of the album, then fold and glue the raw edges to the inside. Glue lengths of ribbon or decorative trim over the raw edges of the pillowcase.
3. We laced a length of ribbon through the existing eyelets on the envelope-style closure of our album.

PLAYFUL PLANTERS
Pages 86-87

1. Paint the rim of a clay flowerpot with a base coat of white acrylic paint and allow to dry.
2. Randomly place ³/₄" round stickers on the surface, pressing firmly to be sure the edges adhere.
3. Paint the rim with a second color and allow to dry.
4. Use the tip of a craft knife to carefully lift the edges of the stickers; remove stickers.
5. Apply two coats of sealer to the painted surface.

CRYSTAL CLEAR
Pages 90-91

1. Re-thread a vintage necklace with a length of wire (to avoid heat damage from the candle's flame, leave a gap in the beads at the top of the hanger by cutting the wire longer than your necklace).
2. Wrap the wire ends around the handles of the sugar bowl, twisting the wire around itself to secure.
3. Place a tea light or small votive candle in the sugar bowl.

Ready to
redecorate?
Check the
recycle bin!

When you see your world through Eco-Chic eyes, recycling becomes much more than putting your bottles and cans on the curb. That's because you know the secrets to making castoffs desirable again. In fact, you'll have so much fun creating beautiful new things out of old containers, dishes, papers, and accessories that you may forget this way of decorating is very green!

re-CYCLE

For centuries, decorator fabrics with pastoral scenes were used for everything from sofas to curtains, but *toile de Jouy* isn't just a patterned fabric anymore. These flea market beauties got their new vistas from wallpaper!

After painting the furniture, we cut pre-pasted wallpaper pieces to cover selected areas. We moistened and smoothed the wallpaper into place and added new drawer pulls to the dresser. These secondhand furnishings gained grand new horizons in a weekend!

Tip: To center your wallpaper scenes, use a single layer of tissue paper to cut a pattern slightly smaller than the area to be covered. You'll be able to see the motif through the tissue paper as you mark the wallpaper for cutting.

take the
SCENIC ROUTE

Some advertisements call for special treatment. To match the stainless-steel cabinets in a retro kitchen, this ad for an innovative line of break-resistant dinnerware needed a sleek metallic frame. Custom framing is worth the expense when the results are this satisfying!

It's easy to "ad" a touch of 20th-century daily life to your kitchen. Advertisers have promoted their goods in magazines for decades, giving us a wealth of resources for fun works of art. You only have to visit a flea market or a pack rat's attic to find these memorable pages from the past, as well as the frames to hold them.

Here's an idea that may help you when you're gathering framing materials: If you have the perfect ad but haven't yet found its frame, go ahead and have mats cut with 4" borders. When the right frame comes along, all you have to do is trim the mats to fit it. The flat wooden frame (top right) was a lucky find — with fabric strips glued on its borders, it coordinates perfectly with the ad and the mats.

it all
"ADS" UP!

Long stitches of red embroidery floss frame an arrangement of colorful buttons. Once the tails of the four lengths of floss are tied together at each corner, this box pillow is complete.

An old container of buttons can bring out the kid in anyone. After all, it's fun to run your fingers through the buttons just to hear them click together. It's even more fun to find a use for the ones that catch your eye. For starters, sew them to purchased pillows or use them to create a new lamp.

For a quick project, simply fill a tall bottle with an assortment of buttons, and then add a bottle adapter lamp kit and a lampshade. You get a new light and your button collection gets a new life.

A bead-fringed pillow is spot-on with a cool collection of black buttons, and it's all "sew" easy!

out of the box
BUTTONS

Fred:

Feed chickens

Milk Cow

Paint Barn

Take note of this trio of flea market fix-ups! A coat of chalkboard paint and a tin sign transform a large baking sheet (opposite, far left) into a message center.

An old cookie sheet (opposite, top) and an enameled pan lid (opposite, bottom) become instant memo boards when you drill holes in two corners to hang them with cord or ribbon. For the magnetic memo minders, search old magazines for pictures and sewing baskets for buttons to glue to craft magnets.

a new recipe FOR NOTES

There's no containing the excitement — metal canisters are truly fabulous finds! Leave them plain to show off their brushed aluminum finish, or use paint to give your storage set retro charm.

To paint the containers, just tape off the knobs and spray on a coat of primer. Paint the dry canisters with black and then green acrylic paint. Sand lightly with fine sandpaper to reveal the paint underneath and create an aged look. For the labels, photocopy the designs on page 157. Cut out the labels and adhere them to the canisters. Your set is complete!

Above, we used a vintage tablecloth to top the lid of this fun cookie tin — without cutting up the cloth! Want to know the secret? Turn to page 146 for the instructions.

little kitchen HELPERS

Take your enamelware collection outside — with this wonderful waterfall of stacked enamelware (upper left). Turn to page 146 for all the how-to's.

This clever towel holder (left) was made using an enamelware pot lid, a plate hanger, a crocheted doily, and ribbon. Leaving a loop at the bottom for hanging a towel, thread a length of ribbon through the handle and tie it into a bow. Glue a length of ribbon to the back of the lid and the doily. To hang, use the plate hanger for the lid and a nail for the doily.

Put a lid on time with this enamelware clock (lower left). Simply remove the knob from a pot lid and insert a purchased clock kit in the hole. **Voilà!** Instant clock.

Above, an enamelware pail makes a handy ice bucket. Stock it with plenty of thirst-quenching beverages to share — you never know who might drop by for a visit.

enamored with
ENAMELWARE

There's simply no improving on a bouquet of Nature's sweet blossoms … or is there? Can you tell which of these arrangements in flea market jars is a gathering of fool-the-eye silk blossoms? Believe it or not, all of these "fresh" cut flowers are artificial and so is the crystal-clear "water"!

You can purchase clear floral setting resin from craft or home decorating stores to make an everlasting silk bouquet of your own. The resin hardens as it cures, so you never have to wipe up spills!

beauti-fool
FLOWERS

Are they pot stickers or pan handlers? Whatever you choose to call them, these fun recycled hybrids give new meaning to the term "kitchen garden."

To grow your own, use a drill and a screwdriver to graft an old kitchen container to the end of a freshly painted spindle. Plant something green in the container, then stake the spindle in the ground. A bumper crop of smiles is guaranteed.

kitchen
GARDEN

The conversation is sure to be lively when your guests are greeted by a dish-lined walkway or twinkling candles and vases swaying in the breeze.

To make a charming flowerbed border in an instant, search your cupboards and attic or visit garage sales and junk shops for mismatched china plates. Don't worry if they are chipped … just "plant" the blemishes in the soil.

Looking for a way to recycle glass bottles and jars? A little wire and a few beads will transform those throw-a-ways into fun and functional vessels. Filled with fresh flowers or candles and hung on your front porch or beneath an arbor they will give your home extra sparkle both day and night. Turn to page 146 for all the how-to's.

start a sparkling
CONVERSATION

Just as red roses are linked with love, these little spice bottles are linked with red ribbon. Entwine and knot two lengths of ribbon between each bottle, then tie the ends into bows.

Spice bottles and salt and pepper shakers make versatile vases because they are just the right size to hold short-stemmed blossoms.

Above, purple paint renews a metal spice caddy. Its four matching bottles can be used as individual vases or kept together with the caddy for a combined bouquet.

For a mini table arrangement (opposite, upper left), tie ribbons around the necks of several spice bottles and place them in a glass dish. Or for a larger display, group silver salt and pepper shakers on a cake stand (opposite, upper right).

spice of
LIFE

Treat your dinner guests to a taste of yesteryear — dress your dinner napkins in vintage costume jewelry! Above, add a dangle from a vintage earring to a coiled faux pearl bracelet for an elegant napkin ring.

On the opposite page from left to right: Tie two lengths of narrow ribbon to each end of a beaded choker. Loop the free ends of the ribbons around the napkin and through the shank of a rhinestone button; then tie them into a bow.

The tasseled beauty in the center features an earring and a purchased tassel glued to a short length of wire-edged ribbon. The ribbon ends are glued together to form a ring.

To make the starburst napkin ring, clasp a sparkling brooch over a length of wide satin ribbon; then knot the ribbon ends together around the napkin.

napkin JEWELRY

As you search for candleholder components, don't limit yourself to tableware — the sparkling glass bowl on a painted candle stand is actually a globe from a light fixture. Once your pillar is in place, add more glow around its base with strands of costume jewelry — you've got razzle-dazzle radiance in an instant!

Everything looks beautiful by candlelight, so it makes sense to give your pretty pillars the setting they deserve. For holders that reflect all this loveliness, try a mix-and-match approach to stacking crystal plates with silver trays and dishes.

Leave your pristine pillars unadorned or soften their effect in an instant by adding assorted beads around the base. See page 147 for the easy details.

waxing
ELEGANT

Above, a collection of mismatched wooden shoes makes an interesting wall display. Recycle the shoes into colorful "planters" by filling them with sphagnum moss and tucking in faux flowering bulbs. To hang, nail sawtooth picture hangers to the heels or use silicone adhesive to attach wire loops.

Put a lid on it! A collection of orphaned lids are recycled into a marvelous montage! Some lids are truly works of art, glazed and painted in a maze of intricate designs and colors. Clustered in a wall grouping, they are a kaleidoscopic delight to the eye! To hang, attach loops of wire to the backs of the lids using silicone adhesive.

artful
COLLECTIONS

Need a little help with your entertaining? Don't overlook the ever-faithful tray. To create this beautiful serving piece from a kitchen cabinet door, turn to page 147. It's a great example of how a flea market find can be recycled into an indispensable asset.

tray
CHIC

Family photographs in flea market frames are displayed in a masculine wall grouping. Vintage bowties come out of retirement when used as hangers for the photographs. Simply glue a piece of ribbon or belting to the back of a bowtie and the remaining end to the back of a frame. To hang, tack the bowtie to the wall using a small nail.

Don't throw out that tired old desk and chair — recycle them into a handsome workspace for a home office or study!

Glue photocopies of cigar box labels around the edges of the desktop, drawer front, and chair edge. For a fresh writing surface, glue a piece of leather to the center of the desktop. Cover the raw edges of the leather with gold cord for an attractive finishing touch.

gentleman's
PREFERENCE

Who would have thought that a box purse with a broken hinge could be recycled into a miniature shelf? Just remove the hinges and front cover, and line the bottom with fabric or paper. Attach two sawtooth picture hangers to the back and your shelf is ready to hang!

Why not wrap your gifts or storage boxes in paper from the flea market? It really doesn't matter what your paper's original function was, as long as it's lightweight enough to fold easily, yet opaque enough to cover your box. This roll of rose print paper might have been intended to cover walls, wrap parcels, or line drawers — we're just glad someone saved it all these years!

who would have THOUGHT?

LITTLE KITCHEN HELPERS

Pages 122-123

1. Remove the lid of a decorative tin and mask off any handles.
2. Spray the container with primer, then with several coats of white spray paint. (We left the lid of our tin its original color.)
3. Color copy a portion of a vintage floral tablecloth, then cut a piece of the copy to fit the lid. Copy the "Cookies" label, page 157. Apply a coat of clear sealer to both sides of the copies.
4. Use découpage glue to adhere the copies to the container and lid and as a sealer to protect the surfaces.

Tip: The same look can be achieved by using color photocopies on self-adhesive paper. No need for glue, simply cut out the labels and smooth in place.

ENAMORED WITH ENAMELWARE

Pages 124-125

To make a dishpan fountain you will need to use $1/2$" diameter galvanized plumbing pieces throughout: three 4"-long nipples, four 90° elbows, one lavatory faucet, one female straight connector, one hose barb, one nipple the desired height for your fountain, and an indoor/outdoor fountain pump that is the size needed to operate your fountain.

1. Use the connector to connect the faucet to the nipple that is the desired height for your fountain.
2. Referring to the diagram, assemble the remaining nipples and elbows into a freestanding base for your faucet; thread the hose barb into the last elbow. Position the faucet base in the dishpan.

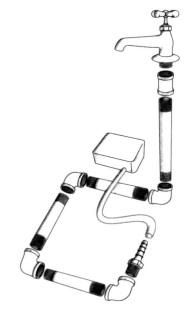

3. Follow the fountain pump manufacturer's instructions to install pump in bottom of pan and to connect plastic tubing to hose barb.
4. Fill the bottom of the pan with rocks for weight. Arrange your enamelware pieces in the pan until they provide the most pleasing sound of trickling water.

TIP: If you're making your fountain a permanent fixture, use clear silicone adhesive to glue your dishware pieces in place.

START A SPARKLING CONVERSATION

Pages 130-131

1. Begin with a generous length of medium-gauge craft wire. Wrap one end of the wire around the top of the

jar and twist the wire around itself to secure. Form a handle the desired length and secure the remaining wire end on the opposite side of the jar; cut away excess wire.

2. To decorate the handle, cut a piece of fine-gauge craft wire that is at least twice the length of the handle. Wrap one end of the wire around the top of the jar several times, adding beads as desired.

3. Adding more beads as you go and ending at the opposite side of the handle, wrap the wire around the handle; twist the wire in place at the end of the handle and cut away excess.

4. To make a beaded dangle, loop and curl one end of a length of fine wire around the wires on the jar. Thread several beads onto the wire, then wrap the wire around and back through the last bead; twist to secure and cut excess.

5. To extend your decorative hanger, cut a piece of medium-gauge wire the desired length for the loop; cut a piece of fine-gauge wire twice as long. Adding beads to fine wire as

desired, wrap the fine wire around the medium wire ... twist the fine wire at the opposite end and cut away the excess. Thread hanger through handle and twist ends at top to secure.

WAXING ELEGANT
Pages 136-137

Turn "pearls" and gold beads from forgotten old necklaces and bracelets into bright, beautiful candle adornments. A scattering of gold seed beads adds extra sparkle.

1. Remove the desired pearls and gold beads from your jewelry pieces.
2. To attach larger pearls, touch the tip of a low-temperature glue gun to the candle to melt a small puddle of wax and press each pearl in place. Cover the candle as desired with larger pearls.
3. To fill in the spaces between the larger pearls, attach smaller pearls, gold beads, and gold seed beads using 1/2" long gold sequin pins.

TRAY CHIC
Pages 140-141

Whether entertaining a crowd or just a few guests, our oversized serving tray provides an elegant touch for your gathering. Your guests will be amazed to discover that this beautiful tray was once a kitchen cabinet door.

1. Cover the door's recessed front panel with a wallpaper remnant.
2. Glue split lengths of bamboo into the routed design which surrounds the panel. To keep bamboo strips from curling away from the tray's surface, place heavy books on the strips until the glue dries.
3. Attach a stylish handle to each end of the tray. Place it on a tray stand or table.

Tip: If you don't have a wallpaper remnant, check out local stores for bargains. Retail stores often offer discontinued or sample wallpaper pieces at discounted prices.

REFINISHING FURNITURE

Cleaning

Often, wiping a piece of furniture down with a clean cloth is all it really needs. If you're simply adding a fresh coat of paint, a light sanding before you prime and paint could do the trick. However, if your piece needs more work, read the following tips before you begin.

• To remove mold or mildew from wood, mix one part household ammonia with nine parts water, then wipe surface with the mixture; wipe away any excess.

• To remove water stains from wood, first try placing a clean, thick cloth over the stain and pressing with a warm, dry iron. Use great care to ensure veneer surfaces do not come loose from any steam action of the iron.

If the stain doesn't disappear, apply a paste wax with 000 steel wool, making sure to rub with the grain of the wood. Continue the wax and steel wool treatment until the appearance of the wood is restored.

Stripping

Chemical strippers vary, so always follow the manufacturer's instructions.

• Apply stripper to a manageable area. Put on a thick coat, and do not disturb it once it is applied.

• After the recommended time, test the finish with a putty knife. The finish should be soft and pliable.

• Carefully using a putty knife, remove as much of the finish as possible.

• Steel wool and bristled brushes often help remove the finish from difficult places.

• Some finishes require multiple applications of stripper.

• Once you have removed as much finish as possible, follow the manufacturer's instructions for cleaning the stripper from the wood.

Sanding

• Following the manufacturer's directions, fill in any nail holes with wood putty to match the piece; lightly sand the areas for a smooth finish.

• Unless you are sanding out imperfections, a simple wipe-down with liquid deglosser is an easy way to prep a surface for priming.

• Sanding with the grain, use a coarse sandpaper to smooth any rough places in the wood, then use a medium grade, and finally a fine grade as needed.

• When working on flat surfaces, wrap the sandpaper around a wooden block to make it easier to hold.

• After sanding, wipe the piece with a tack cloth to remove any dust. If using a water-based finish, however, use a soft dry cloth or vacuum away the dust.

Finishing

• Always read the manufacturer's instructions before applying any stain, paint, or other finish.

• Test any finishing product in a hidden spot, like the back of a drawer before applying to the entire surface.

• Relax — if you don't like how your project turns out, simply start over with a new coat of paint!

DRY BRUSHING

This technique creates a random topcoat coloration of a project's surface. It makes the surface appear aged. Using a dry, clean brush, dip a stipple brush or old paintbrush in paint; brush most of the paint off onto a dry paper towel. Lightly stroke the brush across the area to receive color. Decrease pressure on the brush as you move outward. Repeat as needed to create the desired effect.

PAINTING METAL

1. If your metal item has never been painted, lightly sand the surface using fine sandpaper. If your metal item was previously painted, remove any flaking paint by gently scraping and then sanding the surface.
2. Using a damp cloth, wipe away any sanding residue.
3. Apply a primer designed for metal; allow primer to dry throughly.
4. Apply desired paint color.

AGATE FAUX FINISH

Paint the surface pale grey and allow to dry. Using a dark grey and two lighter shades of grey paint, dip a dampened natural sponge piece into the paint, mixing the colors as you pick up the paint. Blot sponge on a paper towel to remove excess paint, then use a light stamping motion to paint over the basecoat, allowing some of the basecoat to show through. Allow paint to dry. Randomly sponge dark grey paint over the surface and allow to dry. Sponge on a final coat of light grey and allow to dry.

MAKING CLOCKS

Parts for your clock projects are available in kits that include the movement module and hands.

Be sure to measure the thickness of your clock face, as movement modules are manufactured with different shaft lengths.

For a custom look, choose hands and numerals as "separates," sold in a wide array of styles.

To assemble, drill a hole in the clock face large enough for the clock shaft. Follow manufacturer's instructions to attach the movement module and hands.

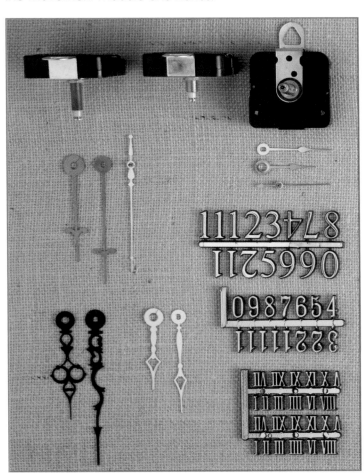

MAKING A BASIC PILLOW

Whether you are converting a framed needlepoint piece into a pillow, making a box cushion, or a chair cover with a ruffle, these basic instructions apply to all the pillows:

1. Use a ½" seam allowance for all sewing unless otherwise indicated.
2. When sewing seams, match the right sides and raw edges.
3. Leave an opening along the bottom edge large enough for turning and inserting fiberfill or a pillow form.
4. After sewing fronts and backs together, turn right side out, carefully pushing corners outward. Insert pillow form, if used, then sew opening closed.
5. Refer to each pillow for specific details.

RUFFLE

1. For the Girly-Girl chair, page 53, use the measurement determined in Step 3 of the Seat Cover instructions. For all other projects, measure the pillow top circumference. Multiply the determined measurement by 2½. Multiply desired finished ruffle width by 2 and add 1" (for example, for a 2" wide ruffle cut a 5" wide strip by the determined length); cut a piece of fabric (piecing if necessary) the determined measurements.
2. Matching right sides, sew short ends together; press the seam allowance open.
3. Matching wrong sides, fold the ruffle in half lengthwise and press. Baste ¼" and ½" from the raw edges of the ruffle. Pull the basting threads to gather ruffle along raw edges, distributing gathers evenly to fit around pillow top. Matching raw edges, baste ruffle to right side of pillow top.

WELTING

Making Welting

1. For the Girly-Girl chair, page 53, use the measurement determined in Step 3 of the Seat Cover instructions. For all other projects, measure the pillow top circumference. Add 1" to the determined measurement. Cut a length of medium diameter cotton cording this length. Cut a bias strip of fabric (piecing if necessary) the same length as the cording and wide enough to wrap around cording plus 2".
2. Center cording on the wrong side of the bias strip; fold strip over cording. Use a zipper foot to machine baste along the length of the strip close to the cording. Trim the seam allowance to ½".

Attaching Welting

1. Beginning at center bottom and matching raw edges, pin welting to the right side of the pillow top, clipping seam allowances as needed to turn corners.
2. Starting 1" from one end of the welting, baste welting to the right side of your pillow top, stopping 2" from other end. Cut welting so ends overlap by 1".
3. Remove 1" of basting from one end of welting. Holding fabric away from cord, trim cord ends to meet exactly. Turning one end of welting fabric under ½", insert one end of welting into the other; baste in place.

Fig. 1

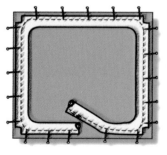

Fig. 2

COVERING A BOX LID

1. Cut a piece of fabric large enough to cover the lid. Center the lid on the wrong side of the fabric and draw around the lid.
2. Use a ruler to draw lines 1/2" outside the drawn lines, extending lines to edges of fabric. Draw diagonal lines from the intersections of the outer lines to the corners of the original lines.
3. Cut away the corners of fabric and clip along the diagonal lines (Fig. 1).

Fig. 1

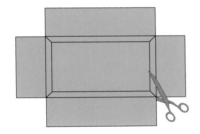

4. Apply spray adhesive to the wrong side of the fabric.
5. Center the lid on the fabric, matching the lid to original drawn lines; smooth the fabric on the top of the lid.
6. To cover the sides of the lid, smooth the fabric onto the sides of the lid. Smooth the excess fabric around the corners onto the adjacent sides. Smooth the fabric to the inside of the lid, clipping as necessary (Fig. 2).

Fig. 2

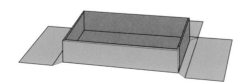

7. To cover each end, smooth the fabric onto end of the lid. Use a craft knife and ruler to trim the excess fabric even with the corners. Smooth the fabric to the inside of the lid.

COVERING FOAM CORE OR POSTER BOARD WITH FABRIC

1. Cut a piece of foam core or poster board to fit desired space.

2. Draw around the piece on the wrong side of your selected fabric; cut out 1" outside the drawn lines.

3. Clipping the fabric as necessary, use thick craft glue or spray adhesive to cover poster board or foam core with fabric and to adhere the fabric panel to the project.

MAKING A CUSHION WITH FOAM AND FABRIC

1. Cut a piece of foam the size needed for your project. **Tip:** To cut through thick pieces of foam quickly and easily, use an electric knife. For added stability, you may want to back your foam with a piece of plywood cut the same size as your foam.

2. Cut a piece of batting large enough to cover the foam and wrap around to the wrong side of the foam. Cut a piece of fabric large enough wrap around to the wrong side of the foam and overlap at center bottom.

3. Center batting, foam, and plywood (if used) on the wrong side of the fabric.

4. If you are using wood backing, wrap the edges of the batting over the foam and wood and staple in place.

5. Wrap the edges of the fabric over the foam, batting, and wood, folding the ends gift-wrap style and stapling in place as you go. **Tip:** To create a nice finished edge, fold or press one long edge of your fabric to the wrong side before securing in place.

6. If you are not using a wood backing, wrap the batting and fabric around the foam gift-wrap style and sew or safety pin the edges of the fabric in place at the bottom of the cushion.

COVERING A CHAIR SEAT

1. Remove the seat from the chair. Draw around the seat on the wrong side of the fabric. Cut out the fabric 3" outside drawn line. Cut a piece of batting the same size as the seat. (You may need to cut several layers of batting for desired thickness of seat.) Layer the batting, then the seat on the wrong side of the fabric.

2. Pulling the fabric taut, staple the center of two opposite fabric edges to the bottom of the seat.

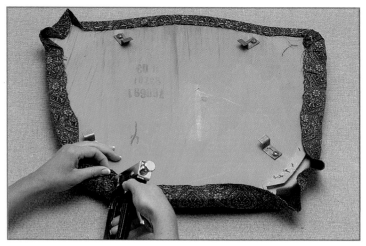

3. Repeat with the other two edges. Work from the center to the corners, stretching the fabric evenly and rotating the seat to the opposite side after each staple.

4. Staple the fabric at the center of each corner, then ease and staple the fabric around the rest of the corner.

COVERING A LAMPSHADE

Note: Self-adhesive shades come with a paper cover that can be used as a pattern. If you are using one of these shades, skip to Step 3.

1. To make a pattern, find the seamline of the shade or use a ruler to lightly draw a vertical line from the top edge to the bottom edge. Place one edge of a piece of tissue paper along the seamline and use removable tape to hold it in place. Wrap the paper tightly around the shade and tape to secure. Use a ruler to draw a vertical line on the paper, 1″ beyond the seamline for the overlap.

2. Draw lines along the top and bottom edges of the shade to complete your pattern. Leaving the first edge of the paper taped to the shade, untape the overlapping edge and finish drawing lines along the top and bottom of the paper. Remove the paper from the shade and cut out the pattern along the drawn lines.

3. Draw around the pattern on the wrong side of your fabric and then cut the cover from the fabric. Press one short end of the cover ¹/₂″ to the wrong side.

4. Apply spray adhesive to the wrong side of the cover. Beginning with the unpressed end along the seamline and aligning the top and bottom edges, center the cover on the shade; gently ease the cover around the shade, adhering it to the shade and smoothing toward the edges. Glue the pressed end in place.

5. To add decorative trim to cover the raw edges, cut a length of trim to fit along the top and/or the bottom edges of the shade; beginning and ending at the seamline, glue the trim in place.

MAKING CANDLES

The following are only intended to be general guidelines for candle making and may not apply to the particular product you are using. Always follow your wax or gel manufacturer's instructions for working with their product.

Working With Wax

Caution: Do not melt wax over an open flame or in a pan placed directly on a burner.

1. Cover your work area with newspaper.

2. Cut a length of wick at least 2″ longer than the height of your mold. Anchor one end of the wick to the bottom of your mold with a wick sticker or drop of hot glue. Some wicks come pre-cut and have sticky tabs for securing them in the molds.

3. In a saucepan, heat 1″ of water to boiling. Add water as needed.

4. Place candle wax in a large can. Pinch the top of the can to form a spout.

5. Place the can in the boiling water and reduce heat to simmer. To keep bubbles from forming in your finished candle, stir only if necessary.

6. If desired, add candle dye or fragrance; stir gently.

7. Holding wick upright, pour wax into molds.

8. Allow wax to harden; trim wick to about ¹/₂″.

Working With Gel

Caution: Avoid using very thin glassware for your candleholders as hot gel may cause breakage.

1. Cover your work area with newspaper.

2. Cut a length of wick at least 2″ longer than the height of your container. Anchor one end of the wick to the bottom of your mold with a wick sticker or drop of hot glue. Some wicks come precut and have sticky tabs for securing them in the container.

3. Cut gel into cubes and place in a saucepan.

4. Using a candy thermometer, melt gel to 225° over a low to medium heat. Gel will melt slowly, do not use a higher temperature.

5. If desired, add candle dye or fragrance; stir gently.

6. Holding wick upright, pour gel into container.

7. Allow gel to harden; trim wick to about ¹/₂″.

FLOUR

SUGAR

COFFEE

TEA

BREAD

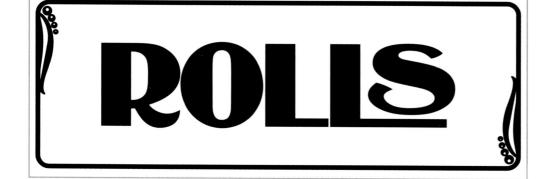

ROLLS

COOKIES

Field Lark.

L'Hotel du Majorque

35 Rue d'Orleans

Paris